When Faith Says Move

When Faith Says Move

A Woman's Guide to Moving Past Worry and Frustration
While Grasping an Understanding of Self-Worth

By

DEIDRA BARNES

ISBN: 9781676474067 (paperback)

Dedication

This book is dedicated to the Lord Jesus Christ. Thank you for giving me the vision and endurance to complete the task you gave me. You are faithful, and your word is true. Your promises are present, and your love is everlasting. Thank you for thinking of me on the cross!

Love,

Dee

Table of Contents

Preface

Elementary school was the best time of my life! I still know the exact feeling I would get as my best friend and I would watch the clock, waiting for my teacher to say, "Okay class, put your notebooks away, and I'll be calling quiet tables to line up for recess." Oh, how I wish fourth grade would return, when fitting in was not as important, when opinions did not matter as much, and when Barbie and Bratz dolls trumped impressing a group of friends. I call it childhood.

My favorite thing about being a teacher is watching the kids at recess. It's the time of day when students forget about what happened during lunch, what happened before they left the house, or what happened during specials. It's the time of day when students release residual anger, doubt, fear, guilt, insecurity, and pain, and they boldly run in freedom without looking back. The smiles come back, the joy is present, and all negativity is lost.

When I got to middle school, I noticed I was different. Do you know the awkward phase preteens and teenagers go through, when pimples and braces become your life? That was me, and we called it the "duck" stage. For the longest time, I could not understand why I wasn't accepted by the popular crowd. Why couldn't I ever get a date for a dance, sit at the popular table without getting "roasted," or hang out with the pretty girls who wore makeup? I just wanted to be their friend. It wasn't until my mother told me, "Deidra, everyone in life is not going to be your friend, and you need to learn that quick, fast, and in a hurry."

The idea of fitting in ruled my mind but then I realized you can't fit in when you're called to stand out. This thought followed me throughout high school and college and even into the workforce. The thing is, I didn't know how to stand out or what made me stand out. Could it be that I was cut from a different cloth? Could it be that my life had more meaning than others' opinions? How could I overcome the internal tug? For years I struggled with insecurities, both internally and externally. I felt as if I was not smart or pretty enough. For years I struggled with depression because my identity was wrapped up in relationships and materialistic items that contorted my mind. The question that constantly came to me was, "Who am I?" The hardest part about asking the question was the fact that I couldn't answer it. I was lost until, one day, I decided to be bold and ask for help. That's when I knew the hardest part was no longer not being able to answer the question. The hardest part was trying to do it on my own. When I approached the throne boldly and told the Lord exactly why I was coming to Him, He began to peel back the layers in my life like an onion.

This book was designed to help women see their true worth in Christ. It is time to stop letting others' opinions define us and know who we always were in Christ. This book will allow you to take a deep look inside yourself to address hidden insecurities, doubts, and fears while breaking free of a stronghold that was conquered on Calvary's cross. With the help of Christ and complete transparency, we will go on a faith quest together, looking at our lives and how they are parallel to those of people in the Bible. It is my vision to see you overcome internal battles and come out on top, knowing that you have been liberated through Christ Jesus. By the end of this book, make it your personal mission to release the trauma and walk triumphantly to the throne.

How To Use This Book

Welcome to When Faith Says Move: I pray that this book touches your heart and will allow you to grow in a deeper relationship with our Creator, God! This book is broken into six units where you will be challenged to self-reflect. Each unit is comprised of different interactive activities that are intended to draw you closer to the Lord. While this book is designed as a Bible Study from different stories in the Bible and real-life examples, you will also be challenged to read and meditate on the scriptures within each unit.

It is the intent to grow from just being hearers of the word-to also being doers of the word! May your experience be full of joy and hope, and may it equip you to impact the world one person at a time.

UNIT 1

Fear, Fearful, Fearfully

Unit 1

Fear, Fearful, Fearfully

One of my favorite radio stations to listen to is 94.1 "The Fish." The top song that I always hear and have completely fallen in love with is a song that focuses on fear. As a woman, I've noticed there are many times when I'm walking in fear, but the question that is hard to answer is, why? Being entangled with fear seems to paralyze us, and the majority of the time, we cannot see the damage until circumstances cause us to move. For most of my life, I've struggled with the opinions of others. I wasn't the average kid. While some kids are afraid of realistic things that can be seen, I was on the other end of the spectrum. I was afraid of the things that could not be seen or heard. In middle school, I was always afraid of not fitting in. I was constantly worried about how I looked, how I dressed, my shoes, my hair, and my height. Anything that could go through the mind of a preteen was going through mine. I think the things that bothered me the most were the things I couldn't change at all.

As I got older, I realized my fear stemmed from something greater. I didn't know who I was. I knew my last name, and I knew I liked to play sports and sing, but I didn't know who I was spiritually. Then it hit me. Fear comes when we don't know our worth or the power we have as women through Christ. We can see a lot of similarities between our character traits and Eve's character traits. In Genesis 3, we find the famous story of Adam, Eve, and the fall of humanity. Go ahead and read Genesis 3 in its entirety.

At the beginning of the chapter, we are introduced to three important figures. What does verse 1 (Gen. 3:1, Christian Standard Bible) say?

Now the _____ was the most _____ of all the wild animals that the _____ _____ had ____ _____. He said to the _____, "Did God really say, 'You can't eat from any tree in the garden'?"

List the three figures that are introduced in verse 1:

1.
2.
3.

In fourth grade, one of the English Standards that students are taught deals with character traits. When I teach character traits, I always tell my students to look at how people are acting and responding. Read verses 1–6, and based on what you read, I want you to write down any character traits you notice about each person.

Person	Character Trait(s)
Serpent	
God	
Eve	

There are major character traits that can be taken from each person, some that are red flags and some that are piles of gold. When I looked up the definition of a serpent[1], Webster gave many

---

[1] Serpent. In *The Merriam-Webster.com Dictionary*. Retrieved January 24, 2020, from https://www.merriam-webster.com/dictionary/serpent

examples, such as a snake or a treacherous person. The serpent in the bible not only represents a physical animal in the context it's being used in, but it also represents character traits of the enemy himself.

My mother is absolutely terrified of snakes. She can't stand them! I remember one time in my biology lab, we got an opportunity to hold a snake, and of course, being the mischievous child I was, I sent her a picture of me holding the snake. That didn't end well! Sometimes snakes are known to take what doesn't rightfully belong to them. When I look at the character traits of the serpent, I see that he is sneaky and convincing. I see that God is all-knowing, and I see that Eve is unsure and naive.

In taking a closer look at Eve, I think it's safe to say that Eve originally knew her purpose, but she misplaced it when she was captivated by distractions. It's like the old saying, "Don't tell me how to take care of my garden when you have weeds in yours." So many times, we as women know what we are supposed to be doing, but distractions come our way and lead us down a path of paranoia instead of precision.

I was once giving directions in my class, and I watched as one student was off task, playing in his desk. I knew for a fact this student didn't hear a word I was saying. One of his peers sitting at his table decided to correct him, and in the other student's correcting, they both ended up missing the directions. I watched both students as it was time to execute the directions. They were as lost as stray puppies. This reminds me of us at times; we know exactly what God wants us to do, but we miss the full directions because we get distracted with what's around us, whether that's a distraction with relationships, friendships, work, or comparisons. These distractions cause us to lose focus and operate in paranoia, where we end up having irrational suspiciousness with what we originally heard from the Lord. Can I tell you that the Lord wants His daughters to operate in precision? When we know who we are, we can be accurate with our tasks—boldly.

Eve had a purpose and knew her purpose! Please read Genesis 1:26–28 (CSB) and fill in the words of each scripture below.

Verse 26: Then God said, "Let ____ make man in _____ _____, according to _____ likeness. _____ will _____ the fish of the sea, the birds of the sky, the livestock, the whole earth, and the creatures that crawl on the earth."

Verse 27: So God _____ _____ in his own image; he created him in the _____ of _____; he created _____ male and _____.

Verse 28: God _____ them, and God said to them, "Be _____, _____, _____ the _____, and _____ it. Rule the fish of the sea, the birds of the sky, and every creature that crawls on the _____."

As you read through these scriptures, you may have noticed many plural pronouns, such as *us*, *they*, *our*, and *them*. These words are important because they help us to see that we are made in the image of the Father, the Son, and the Holy Spirit. It also helps us to see that the word *man* used in this scripture represents all humanity, men and women. Eve was given power and authority through the Lord. God made it very clear who she was (a daughter made in His image) and what she was to do (be fruitful and multiply, fill the earth, and subdue it). You might be saying, "Wait! How did Eve have a purpose before she was even taken from Adam's rib?" My Bible scholar, I'm glad you asked. The Lord created Adam and Eve in chapter 1 of Genesis, but He didn't breathe life into them until chapter 2. Please read Genesis 2:7 and 2:22.

What did God do to man in Genesis 2:7?

A) Delivered him from evil
B) Saved him from drama
C) Formed him from dust

After God formed man, scripture follows up with saying that God breathed the breath of life in his nostrils, and he became a living being.

How did God create the woman in Genesis 2:22?

A) He spoke
B) He took a rib from man
C) He made her out of clay

Before we move on to our next section, I want you to meditate on what your purpose is. Who are you? What is it God is calling you to do? Take the time to think about these questions. God created you with love, and you are His daughter! It reminds me of Psalm 139:13, where the Psalmist says, "For it was you who created my inward parts; you knit me together in my mother's womb" (CSB).

My purpose is...

_____

_____

_____

_____

_____

_____

_____

_____

_____

Paranoia versus Precision

I remember when my then fiancé and I were driving to Arkansas to visit his family for Memorial Day. As we were driving down the two-lane highway, we noticed that at some points, the road looked as if it had water on it. It's something many of us have seen and heard of, and it's called a mirage. The way the light was reflecting on the ground made it look like water. I'm thankful my high school physics came in handy! There wasn't real water on the ground, but my eyes saw something completely different from what was there, which led me to believe that water was in a place where it truly wasn't. We can see these same illusions with Eve in Genesis 3. Eve knew the word of God, but she relied on her own strength and saw something to be desirable that wasn't intended for her. Please read Genesis 2:16–17. While reading the scripture, pay attention to whom the directions are being given.

What is the command that the Lord gave to Adam?

_____

_____

The Lord gave Adam the freedom to eat from any tree in the garden except the tree of the knowledge of good and evil. There are several words in that scripture that help us understand that God means business! In the fourth grade, students learn modal auxiliary verbs. These verbs are used to help the kids differentiate between a possibility, a permission, or an obligation. Use the chart below to help you find the modal auxiliary verbs in Genesis 2:16–17. Highlight and underline as needed.

Word Bank
may   might   shall   will must   could   can   should
Gen. 2:16–17 (CSB) And the Lord God commanded the man, "You are free to eat from any tree of the garden, but you must not eat from the tree of the knowledge of good and evil, for on the day you eat from it, you will certainly die."

If you selected words such as *must* and *will*, you get 100 percent! In the New King James (NKJ) translation, the words *may* and *shall* are used. My Bible scholar, you have mastered modal auxiliary verbs. We read that Adam has been commanded by the Lord, and naturally, he passes the information to Eve. Now, I know in the back of your head you are wondering, "How do we know he gave her the information?" I'm glad you asked; let's look at this together. Here is where the paranoia comes in. Read Genesis 3:2–6.

In those verses, we see that Eve is now having a conversation with the serpent about the instructions she was given; however, when she responds, she misquotes the Lord's instructions, and that gives leeway for the enemy to come in. Eve tells the serpent in verse 3 that she can't eat from the tree or touch it. God did not say anything about touching the tree. He told them not to eat from the tree. Remember, earlier we saw what the Lord commanded the man in Genesis 2:16–17. Eve, in misquoting the Lord, showed the serpent that she was not certain of the word of God. Have you ever been tempted to think differently about God's word or think that His word might not apply to you? I remember when I was having trouble at a job. I felt that I was constantly being ridiculed in meetings. I knew the Lord said in Hebrews 13:5–6 that He will never leave me nor forsake me and that I can boldly say, "The Lord is my helper. I will not be afraid. What can man do to me?" (Heb. 13:6, CSB), but I felt as if the scripture did not apply to me. I was frustrated, and quite honestly, I was seeking answers from the Lord.

An acronym I use that vividly depicts how the enemy attacks children of God is STOP. The enemy attacks when we are Seeking, Thinking, Open, and giving Permission. Thinking back on my situation at work, I was *seeking* acceptance and answers, and I was *open* and vulnerable to having negative thoughts about myself. This led me to briefly believe that God's word had an error. Thank God I have a sister in Christ who held me accountable. My friend would always tell me, "God's word never returns void!" Can you think of a time when the enemy attacked you when you were seeking something, thinking about change, open to vulnerability, or giving the enemy permission to come in your heart?

❑ Seeking

_____
_____
_____
_____

❑ Thinking

_____
_____
_____
_____

❑ Open

_____
_____
_____
_____

❑ Permission

_____
_____
_____
_____

One thing I noticed about the enemy is that he truly focuses on our areas that are weaker than others. In verse 6, there are key words that signal which phase Eve was being tempted in. Please read Genesis 3:6 (CSB) and fill in the blanks with the correct words:

The woman _____ that the tree was good for _____ and _____ to _____ at, and that it was _____ for obtaining wisdom. So she took some of its _____ and _____ it; she also gave some to her husband, who was with her, and he _____ it.

These words scream "seeking"! In verse 6, there is a lot of symbolism for seeking to please sinful desires. Naturally, when we are hungry, like Eve, we look to please our desires with something that can be consumed, whether physically or spiritually. What if our desires with sin work the same way? Can I challenge you as women in Christ to survey your soul? Whenever you feel tempted, I want you to think about what category in your life is being attacked. Is it when you're seeking, thinking, open, or giving permission? When those temptations creep in, fight them with the word of the Lord. Remember, you have a purpose and authority.

Write a prayer to the Lord focusing on the area you want to be strengthened in:

_____
_____
_____
_____
_____
_____
_____
_____
_____

Stop Running

We are now to the part of our study where we are introduced to the first sign of fear in the Bible. I know I've mentioned what scares my mother and what scares me, but what about you? In this section, we are going to focus on what fear is, what it causes us to do, and how we can overcome it. The key during this section is to be honest with ourselves and the Lord. When we try to overcome fear by our own power, we become captive to it every time. To begin our study, please read Genesis 3:7–13.

Boy oh boy, are they in trouble! As I said, we can see a lot of character traits within ourselves and other people in the Bible. My brother and I have always been extremely close. We are thirteen months apart, but we grew up like twins. I can specifically remember a time when my brother and I got in trouble with my daddy. We were supposed to be raking the leaves, and a simple leaf fight had turned into a physical fight. This would always disappoint my parents, because they instilled in us the importance of family. When it was time for my brother and me to face my daddy and tell the truth, we both tucked our heads down and looked at the ground. Silence. We were ashamed to tell my daddy the truth, and as a response to feeling guilt and shame, we hid from the truth. When Adam and Eve sinned in the garden, they were exposed to good and evil. Instead of then running to their Father and telling Him the mistake they made, they hid from Him.

Something interesting happens in verses 9–10. God and Adam are having a conversation, and God says something that might cause many heads to turn: "Where are you?" This simple question is being asked by an all-knowing God, but the question poses a deeper meaning that we can apply to our lives, as well. God wanted Adam to check his position in his heart and in his relationship with Him. This rhetorical question that the Lord asked Adam can also be asked of us. I want you to think about your personal relationship with the Lord. Using the scale, I want you to draw where your actual relationship lands, and where you desire your relationship to be with the Lord.

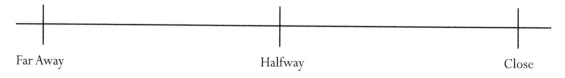

Far Away   Halfway   Close

The closer we are to the Lord, the more we understand His true love for us. Because Adam's position was farther away than anticipated, his perception of the Lord changed. We see, for the very first time in the Bible, the word *afraid* used. Steffany Gretzinger has a song called "No Fear in Love." I can imagine this song playing as Adam tells his creator, his Father, that he is afraid of Him. When we make a mistake, our natural reaction is to try and hide the mistake, because we are afraid of letting those closest to us down. Do not get me wrong; the Lord is a good Father, so He does discipline, but His discipline is not given out of scrutiny, it is out of love. He wants His children to grow, learn, and flourish. We serve a God whose love is so vast, so what causes us to be afraid of the One who created us? My Bible scholar, it is something so simple, yet so complex: fear is a spirit. Please read 2 Timothy 1:7.

God has not given us the spirit of

- ❏ Wonder
- ❏ Questions
- ❏ Fear

God has given us the spirit of

- ❏ Power
- ❏ Love
- ❏ Sound Judgment

My love, fear is a spirit that the Lord did not give us. We have power through His name, love through His name, and sound judgment through His name. Having sound judgment means having a clear mind to process information without interruption or altered feelings based on circumstances. As we look further into verses 11–13 of Genesis 3, we see that the spirit of fear causes us to place blame and not take responsibility for our actions. This reminds me of recess time at school. Watching over one hundred children on the playground is a job, but it is so enjoyable…until a group of students come up to you and tell you why their friend is crying his or her eyes out. One year, particularly, there was a lot of girl drama among the fourth-grade classes. One time at recess, a group of about seven girls came to me to tell me why their friend was crying. Being a rookie teacher, I made the biggest mistake I could have made in that moment. I asked the general question, "What happened?" Before I knew it, everyone was yelling at each other and blaming one another for what happened. Not only did they have a screaming match, but they also did not take responsibility for their actions. Have you ever made a mistake and decided to blame it on everything else around you? If so, share your experience below.

_____

_____

_____

_____

_____

_____

_____

One thing I have noticed as a teacher is that grammar is important. There are so many parts to the English language, which is what makes English the hardest language to learn. In order to complete this next activity about yourself, you need to know different parts of speech.

- A noun is a person, place, thing, idea, or animal.
- An adjective describes the noun.
- A verb is an action or, in better terms, something you can do.
- An adverb describes the verb (it usually focuses on how, how often, how much, when, or where).

Here is an example of the parts of speech used in a simple sentence:

Rachel is beautiful when she eagerly looks in the mirror.
Noun   Adjective   Adverb Verb
                        (Describes how)

When we look at the words *fear*, *fearful*, and *fearfully*, we can pull out the same parts of speech. I want you to think about what noun puts fear in you. How would you describe that noun? Please be honest, but also show integrity if you are using a person.

My Fear (Noun)	Describing your fear (Adjective)

Next, I want you to think of an action you can do whenever your fear seems to get in your heart, and describe your action.

My Action (Verb)	How, How Often, How Much, When, Where (will I do this verb)

The Bible tells us in Psalm 23:4, "Even when I go through the darkest valley, I fear no danger, for you are with me; your rod and your staff—they comfort me." God will never fail us, and He will always lead us in the direction we are supposed to go. Whenever you feel fear, I want you to go back to your chart and look at the actions you said you will take. Growing up in my home church in Kansas City, Kansas, I was a member of the Young Women's Society. In that class, our First Lady made it a mission for us to memorize Psalm 139:14, "I will praise you because I have been remarkably and wondrously made. Your works are wonderous, and I know this very well." At first the scripture made no sense to me; however, when I experienced heartbreak, I finally knew what the scripture was saying. I did not have to settle for less any longer. My sister in Christ, I want you to know that you are fearfully and wonderfully made! Going back to our grammar lesson, adverbs describe the action, and my dear, when God created you, He made you remarkably special!

The best thing about being a teacher is the fact that I get to give my students different tools to use when it is time to solve difficult problems. I always tell my students, "I do not care what tool you use, as long as you use at least one." As we bring this unit to a close, I want to leave you with some spiritual tools that you can use whenever you feel fear in your life:

1. Identify what your fears are. It is okay to acknowledge that there are fears present.
2. Be honest with yourself. Why do you have these fears?
3. Ask for help. The majority of the time, you are not alone in your process. Seek wise counsel from someone you trust.

UNIT 2

Preparation for My Destination

Unit 2

PREPARATION FOR MY DESTINATION

Welcome to unit 2! In this unit, we will focus on preparing for the next level in our lives. I ask that as we venture through this segment, you allow your hearts and minds to be shifted by the Lord. We will do a lot of soul-searching and reflection. While this may be a little uncomfortable at first, I want you to rest assured that you will come out a stronger woman than you were when you entered this section. Before we begin this study, I want you to ask the Lord to reveal His will for your life. Write out a prayer that is specific to what you want the Lord to reveal:

_____

_____

_____

_____

_____

_____

_____

_____

_____

_____

_____

_____

My students mastered a reading standard this year that focused on finding the theme of a story. At first, my kids had a difficult time grasping the concept, but after some guidance it became a breeze. When you are finding the theme of a story, you are looking for a moral meaning that you can apply to your life. I told my kids that theme always relates to behavior. The Lord graciously gave me a theme for my life when I was in college. During this time in my life, I was not sure I was going to graduate, and I was processing through the consequences of being unequally yoked in relationships and friend-ships. I kept getting attacked by the enemy with a word called *doubt*. This word will cause you to walk in fear based on five subgroups. Whenever you feel doubt encroaching, I want you to think of these things: Distance, Obligation, Uncertainty, Belief, and Time. We begin to doubt when

1. the distance of our dream is unseen,
2. we are overwhelmed by obligations,
3. we are uncertain of our dreams,
4. our situations contradict our beliefs, or
5. we are pressed for time.

Have you experienced a time when you started doubting? Use the chart to give an example of each subgroup based on your personal experience.

D	O	U	B	T

There's a story in the Bible about someone who experienced doubt, as well. His name was Thomas. Please read John 20:24–29.

This story is notoriously known as Doubting Thomas's story. The disciples have gathered and are discussing how they saw Jesus after His resurrection. Thomas used really strong words in verse 25. Complete the rest of the scripture.

John 20:25, CSB: So the other disciples were telling him, "We've seen the Lord!" But he said to them, "If I don't _____ the mark of the nails in his hands, _____ my finger into the mark of the nails, and _____ my hand into his side, I will _____ believe."

Thomas would definitely ace our grammar skills lesson. He used so many verbs in his statement, but his verbs actually tell us why he was doubting. He needed to see and touch Jesus in order to believe. How many times have we doubted Jesus because we can't see Him? The beautiful thing about our Savior is that He will remind us of His goodness even when it's hard for us to see it. He was so patient with Thomas and allowed him to see His marks, but He needed to inform Thomas on the importance of faith. In verse 27, Jesus tells Thomas, "Don't be faithless, but believe" (John 20:27, CSB). That's what I want you to remember, Bible scholar: your belief in Jesus and what He can do is greater than what you'll ever see with the physical eye. Jesus said Himself in verse 29, "Because you have seen me, you have believed. Blessed are those who have not seen and yet believe." I want you to open your toolbox and make room for more spiritual tools that you're going to add today! Use the following tools when you feel DOUBT:

1. When the distance of your dream is unseen, I want you to know the word of God says in Matthew 28:20, "I am with you always, to the end of the age" (CSB).
2. When you are overwhelmed by obligations, I want you to know the word of God says in John 15:16, "You did not choose me, but I chose you. I appointed you to go and produce fruit and that your fruit should remain, so that whatever you ask the Father in my name, he will give you" (CSB).
3. When you are uncertain of your dreams, I want you to know the word of God says in 2 Peter 1:3, "His divine power has given us everything required for life and godliness through the knowledge of him who called us by his own glory and goodness" (CSB).
4. When your situations contradict your beliefs, I want you to know the word of God says in Romans 10:9, "If you confess with your mouth, 'Jesus is Lord,' and believe in your heart that God raised him from the dead, you will be saved" (CSB).
5. When you are pressed for time, I want you to know the word of God says in Isaiah 44:6, "I am the first and I am the last. There is no God but me" (CSB).

These tools serve as a mechanism to help you when time seems a little unbearable. When I was experiencing a traumatic breakup, I lost hope. I left the door wide open for the enemy to try to steal my identity, kill my purpose, and destroy my self-confidence and self-worth. Just as much as you and I have jobs as warriors in Christ, the enemy has a job, too. It's up to us whether we let the enemy in or let our Savior in! John 10:10 states, "A thief comes only to steal and kill and destroy. I have come so that they may have life and have it in abundance."

The Lord does not want His children to lose hope or walk away empty-handed. When I was going through my breakup, my identity was wrapped up in the relationship. When the relationship ended, I didn't know who I was. I am so thankful for the Holy Spirit comforting me during that difficult time. His soft words spoke to my heart and told me to read Matthew 19:16–22, and my friend, I'm going to ask you to read the same thing in its entirety.

Who are the main characters in the text? Check all that apply.

- ❏ Joseph
- ❏ Michael
- ❏ Jesus
- ❏ Rich young ruler

What was the young man trying to do?

- ❏ Get a ride to the city
- ❏ Go to Jesus's house
- ❏ Have eternal life
- ❏ Give to the poor

If you answered that Jesus and the rich young ruler are the main characters and the young man is trying to see what it takes to have eternal life, you are a rock star! At the end of the story, we note that the young man departs from Jesus crying because he had to let go of some things. This can be characterized in one simple word: *idols.* When the Lord told me to read this story, I couldn't help but cry my eyes out. All these years, I had been acting as the rich young ruler. I wouldn't let go of a relationship that I was idolizing. The Lord's exact words to me were, "So long as you hold onto this relationship, you will never reach your purpose." If I can be quite honest, I was terrified, because that meant God had something greater for me. I was doing everything in my power to hold onto something that wasn't even meant for me, and that was the exact problem. I was operating in my own power, not the power of the Lord. My desires were not in alignment with His will, and I knew I had to drop some baggage to prepare for my destiny.

Name a time when you knew your desires were not in alignment with God's will for your life. How did you drop, or how are you dropping, the baggage to prepare for your destiny?

_____

_____

_____

_____

_____

_____

_____

_____

_____

_____

_____

_____

_____

_____

When I finally decided to prepare for my destination, I felt guilty and ashamed. I felt as if I were not worthy enough to change. I was used to the old me, and shedding away the scales meant I would become new. I'm not sure about you, but I don't do well with change when I can't see the end result. The Lord's word is so reassuring. In 2 Corinthians 5:17 it says, "Therefore, if anyone is in Christ, he is a new creation; the old has passed away, and see, the new has come!" I was free, and it was time to walk in my freedom! My cleansing process was completely dramatic but definitely necessary for me. I wanted the cleansing on the outside to reflect the cleansing that was occurring on the inside. I decided during that time in my life to become a vegetarian and cut my hair off. I wanted my physical body to be in alignment with the change in my spirit and soul.

The renewing of myself was amazing because I realized my body is made up of three parts:

1. My physical body
2. My spirit
3. My soul

If you remember, in unit 1 we learned in Genesis 1:26 that God said, "Let us make man in our image, according to our likeness" (CSB). The plural words *us* and *our* represent the Trinity: the Father, the Son, and the Holy Spirit. Your physical body is a living reminder of how Christ walked this earth. Your spirit is a reminder that you have the Holy Spirit living inside of you, and your soul is a reminder of God, who holds the key to your destiny. Each component of your body has certain subgroups that are equally important. Please look at the diagram below and record your findings. What do you notice, and what connections can you make?

Physical Body	Spirit	Soul

Internal Body	**Mind**	**Immortal**
Heart	Thoughts	Personality
Lungs	Judgement	Character
Organs	Conscience	Identity

External Body	**Will**	
Head	Desires	
Arms	Anticipation	
Legs	Wants	

Emotions

Feelings

_____

_____

_____

_____

_____

_____

_____

_____

_____

_____

_____

_____

_____

_____

Your body is so important, and it is so precious. You were intricately designed, and your body represents more than just you. In better terms, you represent the body of Christ wherever you go. In Romans, Paul is giving believers advice on how to live a solid Christian life. Romans 12:1–2 urges us to present our bodies as a living sacrifice, holy and pleasing to God. He goes on to tell us not to conform to the ways of the world but to be transformed by the renewing of our minds, so that we may be able to discern what is the good, pleasing, and perfect will of God.

Girl, I need you to understand that your body is a temple! A temple is a place where God dwells and where His people worship! In the word of God, 1 Corinthians 6:19 is so powerful. God is giving us a reminder of what our body is. Take a look at the scripture, and write it below.

_____

_____

_____

_____

One group of people whom I love dearly is our elders. They are so honorable and worthy of respect. I love when my grandma visits me. As soon as I get the news that she is on her way, I try to make the house spotless. I could not imagine my grandma staying in a cluttered house. I make sure I take my time to make the bed, vacuum, and make her feel welcome. Is it strange for me to say I view the Holy Spirit the same way? I want Him to live in a clean house, a righteous house. I don't want Him to trip over clutter; I want Him to walk freely and feel welcome. I want you to meditate on your body as a temple. Do you have clutter that you need to get rid of so the Holy Spirit is free to live in you? If so, I want you to write all your clutter on the cross and write a prayer asking the Lord to show you the steps to take in order to rid yourself of the clutter. Your body is a temple!

_____

_____

_____

_____

_____

_____

God prepared so many people in the Bible for their destiny. Each person has his or her own story and own path, but the good thing is seeing how God's love continuously flowed through each situation. As we go through different stories in the Bible leading to individual destinies, I want you to think of all the ways God prepared each person for the next step. We will focus on the destinies of David and Esther. Our first person whom God prepared for his destiny was David. Please read 1 Samuel 17:33–37 and 17:45–51, then complete the chart below using scriptures to support your answers.

Person	Character Trait(s)	Supporting Scriptures
King Saul		
David		
Goliath		

King Saul's comment to David in verse 33 really hit home for me. Even as I am writing this book, I find myself sometimes questioning my gifts because of my age. David was young, but he was anointed by the Lord. You will learn more about David in-depth in the next unit, but until then I want to challenge you to never be intimidated by circumstances because of your age. You have the same power to impact lives as someone who's had more experience in life. In verses 33–37, David was running his credentials, or in better terms, he was telling King Saul all the reasons he was qualified to defeat Goliath, the Philistine. Needless to say, in verses 45–51, David defeated Goliath. The entire time people were doubting David, God was preparing him to fight something bigger than a lion and a bear. As you face the doubting from others, know that like David, God has prepared you for your Goliath by giving you lions and bears to slay.

Our next example is Queen Esther, and our focus scriptures will be Esther 4:14 and 5:1–3. I feel as if we all have something to learn from her, which is the value of resting in the Lord's promise even if things may not go the way we want them to. Here is a summary to catch you up on the book of Esther: a document was signed by the king issuing a command to kill all the Jewish people in the surrounding area; however, Esther was a Jew herself and kept it a secret from the king, her husband… Yes, drama, drama, drama! Fast forward—the Jewish people find out about the document and are horrified. Queen Esther calls for the Jews to fast for three days, consuming no food or water. Early in chapter 5, Esther gains the strength to approach the king. As she approaches him, she gains favor, and he tells her in verse 3, "Whatever you want, even to half the kingdom, will be given to you." Esther had to prepare to see the king by dropping her fear. In the end, as the Lord prepared her heart and words, many people's lives were saved.

As we bring this unit to a close, I want you to remember that preparation for your destination is important. If you have baggage that you need to drop, let it go so the Lord can fully use you without any interruptions. In your own time, I want you to read this prayer and release what is holding you back from your destiny. My sister in Christ, it's time to walk in freedom!

> Lord,
>
> I want to thank You so much for life, family, friends, and fellowship. Today, I want You to search my heart and remove anything in me that is not like You. You created me in Your image, and I am fearfully and wonderfully made. My body is a temple, and I pray that You cleanse me from all impurities. Search my heart and take away my fears, my pain, and my baggage. Lord, I can't hold onto it anymore. You have a purpose for me, and I want to walk in freedom, starting today! Jesus, I thank You for what You are getting ready to do and for what You have already done. Your word is true and never returns void! I ask these blessings in Jesus' name. Amen.

UNIT 3

SEE (Separation, Exposure, Elevation)

UNIT 3

SEE (SEPARATION, EXPOSURE, ELEVATION)

Congratulations, ladies, you are trucking along through this journey, and I can already tell that you've grown so much! In this unit, we will focus on our vision. One thing I've realized about the Lord is that He gives us a glimpse of our future. He helps us to see what's next by giving us insight into ourselves. We are going to have several heart checks during this unit so we can hear God's voice clearly. Before we officially begin, I would like you to write a short note to yourself about what you think your future holds.

_____

_____

_____

_____

If you haven't noticed, I love using acronyms. Not only does it help me remember information, but it also helps me to find a deeper meaning behind concepts. Being born in the 1990s, I've had the privilege to see how things evolved over the years. I vividly remember a toy that my brother and I played with. It was a medium-size cube with different shapes cut out on each side. The purpose of the toy was to help kids match the shapes to the correct side. Every now and then as a kid, I would try to put the triangle where the square was supposed to go, and to my surprise, the triangle wouldn't fit. As I got older, I understood that the same concept applies to our lives. We can't fit in when we are called to stand out. In 2016, I was teaching high school Bible studies, and I always told my kids they were out of the box! Although sometimes being the outcast may feel lonely, that's when we SEE the most.

God's way of helping us SEE requires Separation, Exposure, and Elevation! God has set you apart, or *separated* you, from the world and has appointed you to fulfill His will for your life.

The word *exposure* has such a negative connotation, but in God's eyes, exposure is a key component to growth. God will expose us to ourselves and show us our ashes. The amazing thing about our Savior is that He trades us beauty for ashes. Once we see the areas where God has exposed us to ourselves and we are broken down, the rebuilding process begins, and we are *elevated* to the next level.

I live on the outskirts of Middle Tennessee, and on my way to work, there is a beautiful straightaway that shows farmland on both sides and the horizon in the distance. I would always pass a beautiful brick house sitting on a good amount of acreage, but one day I noticed the house had burned down. I was shocked and felt a wave of sympathy enter into my heart. It was right around Thanksgiving time, and my heart broke for this family. As months progressed, I saw this burned house being torn down to the foundation. At this point, I thought they were going to leave the land as is. Soon after, however, I saw the house being rebuilt. The workers endlessly poured their labor into fixing what was torn down. My sister in Christ, this is a reminder that God is strong enough, wise enough, and good enough to rebuild what was broken.

I want you to think of an area in your life where you feel broken and torn down. Reflect on why you are feeling that way and what you are patiently expecting the Lord to do.

_____

_____

_____

_____

_____

_____

_____

_____

_____

_____

_____

_____

_____

_____

_____

_____

Let's look at David's life more in depth. He got to SEE a glimpse of his future. He experienced separation, exposure, and elevation. Please read 1 Samuel 16:1–13. Once you are finished reading, use the comic strip to draw five important scenes that took place.

A scene that you probably included was Samuel following God's voice to anoint a new king. As Samuel ventured out, he invited Jesse to witness the sacrifice he was making to the Lord. Samuel looked at all of Jesse's sons who were near him and thought the Lord would pick one of them to anoint as the king, but the Lord told Samuel to stop looking at outward appearances, because He looks at the heart. Samuel began to get a little confused, because he was instructed by the Lord to anoint a king, but no one had gained God's approval yet. Samuel decided to ask Jesse if he had another son, and to his surprise, he said yes!

Separation

Poor David. He was an outcast even to his family, and they didn't even think about him until Samuel asked. When David was called in, the Lord quickly told Samuel to anoint him. I can only imagine what David's family was thinking. He was tending to sheep, probably smelled awful, and probably needed a bath. This goes to say that even in the most inconvenient, irrelevant jobs, God still sees you! Do not downplay your position for attention. Whatever job you have, manage it well. God sees you, and He knows you. David was separated from his brothers and was set apart.

Reflection Piece: What have you recently been separated from? What makes you set apart?

_____

_____

_____

In my first year of teaching, a student approached me at recess with a distraught look on her face. When I asked her if she was okay, she proceeded to tell me how she hates not being able to fit in with her classmates. She told me that she didn't know any of the new songs or dances the kids were doing. What opened my eyes was when she asked me if it was a bad thing that she didn't fit in. On the inside, I wanted to cry, because I felt this way as a child growing up. I looked at her and told her it's a good thing that she's different. I explained it to her with an analogy: "Imagine you're in an airplane that's getting ready to land, and right before you touch down, you fly over a field of red roses. As you look closer, you see one white rose in the middle. Which rose will capture your attention?" She told me the white flower would capture her attention, and I told her that she was that white flower and will always be that white flower. The same thing applies to you!

I want you to think of what your field of red flowers is. For some it may be a college campus; for my student it was her peers. For me it was my job. Once you figure yours out, I want you to write a few positive things about the current position you're in. Remember, a huge part of growing is changing your mindset on how you view your situation. Your separation is a season for you to be cultivated into who God wants you to be. Some people around you may take it personally, but know that your separation is a refining process for you! Some may call you stuck up and too good for them, but in reality, you're under construction, honey! God is getting ready to take you to another level.

My current field of red flowers is…
One positive thing about my position is…
Another positive thing about my position is…
The last positive thing about my position is…

Sister, whenever you feel like an outcast, I want you to visit 2 Timothy 1:9, which says, "He has saved us and called us with a holy calling, not according to our works, but according to his own purpose and grace, which was given to us in Christ Jesus before time began" (CSB). God has called you to live out His word, and He has called you to stand out. Keep being a light for the world to see!

Exposure

We learned how David was separated; now let's look at how he experienced exposure. Before we begin, I need you to grab a huge bowl of popcorn! This section gets very messy, but remember, earlier we learned that we serve a Savior who trades us beauty for our ashes. In 2 Samuel 11, we find the story of David's downfall as a king. Previously, we read about how David was anointed as king in his adolescence, but he doesn't live out his anointing until he is an adult. Once David is king, things are going pretty well until he finds a pretty young thing by the name of Bathsheba taking a bath—pun intended. David finds her to be attractive, and they both begin enticing one another, even though she's married. David gets a little beside himself and wants Bathsheba to be his wife, and the only thing standing in the way of their love story is Bathsheba's husband, Uriah. In order for David to carry out his plan of making Bathsheba his wife, he decides to put Uriah on the front line of battle to be killed. David knew exactly what he was doing, but he didn't think twice about it. He was so wrapped up in his own will that he lost sight of God's.

David is then exposed to himself, and it's a hard pill for him to swallow. Please read 2 Samuel 12:1–15.

Who did the Lord send to talk to David?

- ❏ Samuel
- ❏ Uriah
- ❏ Nathan
- ❏ Joab

Why do you think David was furious when Nathan gave him an analogy about a rich man and a poor man?

_____

_____

_____

_____

_____

_____

_____

_____

What four emotions can you use to describe David when he found out he was being compared to the rich man in the story? Why?

1)

2)

3)

4)

_____

_____

_____

David reminds me of the house that burned down in my neighborhood. He was torn down to his foundation. God had to show him his shortcomings so He could fix what was broken. Don't get me wrong—there are definitely consequences for our actions, but God shows us our flaws out of love. When we rely on our own strength, we will hit rock bottom every time. I love 2 Corinthians 12:10, because it is a reassurance that we should delight in our weakness, for when we are weak, we are also strong. Christ's grace gives us strength!

Once a house is torn down to the foundation, the only way to build is up! David has been separated and exposed, but now it is time to see his elevation process. Some of you may be wondering how God can use you after you've done wrong. My answer to that is that His forgiveness is for everyone, including you! We are going to see how David made a tremendous turnaround after he was consumed by his own will.

Elevation

As David's family drama gets juicier, I want you to keep in mind that God still loves him. In 2 Samuel 13–18, everything begins to crumble in David's family. My sister, please brace yourself as I summarize the events that take place in these chapters. You will be able to feel the pain and tension this family is experiencing. Buckle up, ladies, it's going to get wild.

It all begins with David's children, his two sons Amnon and Absalom and his daughter Tamar. Amnon is in love with Tamar and wants to be with her on a deeper level. Amnon decides to play sick and convinces Tamar to bring him food. While she's there, he ends up raping Tamar and throwing her out of his room like trash. Tamar is absolutely devastated, because she was a virgin, so she puts ashes on her head as a symbol of mourning. Tamar tells her brother Absalom, and he tells her to be quiet about the situation because that's her brother. When King David hears about the situation, he is angry but does nothing about it. I don't know about you, but I'm feeling a whirlwind of emotions from this entire situation. Once Absalom sees his father not doing anything about the ordeal, he decides he's going to have his brother Amnon killed. Eventually, after Amnon's death, Absalom rebels against his father and tries to overthrow the throne. In his attempt to take over his father's kingdom, he ends up getting killed himself.

Let's take some time to reflect on the situation that occurred in David's household. What character traits do you think each character has? Fill in the chart below to answer the question.

Person	Character Traits
Amnon	
Absalom	
Tamar	
David	

You may be asking, "Where's the part where things get better?" Things get better in chapter 19 when David's kingdom is restored back to him. He almost lost it when his son was rising against him. The chapter I want you to read is 2 Samuel 22. While you are reading this, I want you to focus on what David is saying.

I can only imagine what David was feeling as he was writing that song to the Lord. David had a lot to get off his chest. He slept with someone's wife and had her husband killed; his son raped his daughter; and in retaliation, his other son killed that son and tried to take over his kingdom. If I had a say, I would say that David was dealing with a lot of guilt, shame, and fear. Even in all of David's mess, God still poured out His love on him. We can see the elevation process in 2 Samuel 22:17–20, where David thanks the Lord for pulling him out of all of his drama and away from his enemies. If God did it for David, He will surely do it for you. No matter what you've done or what's been done to you,

God's purpose still stands in your life. You mean so much to the Lord, sister. Below, I want you to write the portion of David's song that really touched your heart. I challenge you to memorize it and tuck it in a safe place inside.

_____

_____

_____

_____

We got to SEE David's growth. We saw how he was separated, exposed, and elevated. I'm certain David didn't know all of these factors would play into his life, but they did, and the pieces of the puzzle led to a beautiful picture of the gospel of Jesus. Because David was repentant and allowed God to mold him, Jesus was able to come through his bloodline! Before we move on to our last group of individuals who got to SEE their purpose, I want you to complete the chart below on what God wants you to SEE.

Separation [What has God separated you from?]	
Exposure [What has God exposed you to about yourself?]	
Elevation [In what area is God elevating you?]	

Our last group of individuals includes young men who were faced with the idea of compromising their beliefs. For our last study of this unit, we are going to focus on Daniel and the three Hebrew boys whose names were Hananiah, Mishael, and Azariah, or as they were known in Babylon, Shadrach, Meshach, and Abednego. The four young boys go on a forced quest and face adversity throughout their journey. To begin, please read Daniel 1:1–7.

What are the names of the two kings in the story?

_____

_____

What kingdom was King Jehoiakim ruler over?

❏ Babylon
❏ Judah
❏ Turkey

What kingdom was King Nebuchadnezzar ruler over?

❏ Turkey
❏ Babylon
❏ Judah

What did King Nebuchadnezzar take with him back to Babylon?

_____

_____

_____

Now that you know the background of the story, you should have written that King Nebuchadnezzar took gold vessels from the kingdom of Judah, along with many young Israelite boys. Please note, the kingdom of Judah includes the ethnic group of the Israelites. During this time, the kingdom of Babylon was one of the most advanced communities. They were big in art, language, and architecture. They had great music, a lot of parties, and entertainment. I like to consider it as akin to our modern-day New York City. Can you imagine how teenage boys would act if they were away from their parents in a big city like that?

Separation
Daniel, Hananiah, Mishael, and Azariah experienced their first form of separation. They were physically removed from their home environment and forced to learn another culture. The next form of separation these boys experienced was based on their own will. Please read Daniel 1:8–16.

What was Daniel determined about?

❏ Making friends in Babylon
❏ Finding his family again
❏ Not defiling himself

Remember, the Israelites were under a different set of rules than other people. During this time, they were still under the Mosaic law. Thankfully, the New Testament bringing forth the gospel of Christ allowed the Mosaic law to be traded for the cross. 2 Corinthians 5:19 says, "That is, in Christ, God was reconciling the world to himself, not counting their trespasses against them, and he has committed the message of reconciliation to us." (CSB). Christ took the place of the law, and that's something to shout about! While there were so many rules that needed to be followed during that period of time that could easily be broken, on purpose or by accident, Daniel and his friends stayed true to their beliefs and separated themselves from among many.

Exposure

Have you ever been "stuck between a rock and a hard place"? That saying is often used to describe someone who is experiencing a very difficult situation with almost no way out. Hananiah, Mishael, and Azariah were exposed to the public for who they believed in, and it almost cost them their lives… or did it? Please read Daniel 3:4–23.

King Nebuchadnezzar has literally lost his mind. He is so angry at the young men's rebellion in refusing to worship the statue that he decides to throw them in a fiery furnace. In that process, we can see so much symbolism, with God always being by our side in heated situations—literally. I know this situation had to be so worrisome for those around them, but the young men were fine, because they knew who their God was! King Nebuchadnezzar thought he could expose the young men by making an example out of them, but God will always work things in our favor when we love and serve Him.

Elevation

The young men were then elevated later on in the chapter. Please read Daniel 3:24–30.

What was the king astonished at?

_____

_____

_____

_____

Why do you think he was astonished?

_____
_____
_____
_____

Hallelujah! The Lord is always with us in any circumstance we face. He rewards our faithfulness. I want you to look at verse 30. How were Hananiah, Mishael, and Azariah recognized for their faith in the Lord?

_____
_____

Last but not least, we will see how Daniel's experiences are similar to the three Hebrew boys. In Daniel 6, Daniel is set up by people who despise him. Basically, they viewed him as a goody two-shoes, and they wanted to see him fail. They asked the new king during that time, Darius, to sign off on a law that stated the only person the people in the city could pray to was him, and if anyone disobeyed that order they would be thrown into the lions' den. Daniel, being the strong man he was, decided to stick to his beliefs, just as the Hebrew boys did. In return, there were consequences, and he was thrown into the lions' den. The king was really hurt because of this, because he actually liked Daniel as a person. The group that set Daniel up wanted to make an example out of him, as well, but their plan did not work. The Lord sent an angel to shut the lions' mouths. In the end, verse 28 says, "So Daniel prospered during the reign of Darius and the reign of Cyrus the Persian" (Dan. 6:28, CSB). The king saw how mighty Daniel's God was and made it a point to elevate Daniel to the next level.

My friend, this concludes unit 3, but before we move on, I want you to reflect on the next level God is trying to take you to. You may go through a separation. You may be exposed, but one thing remains true. You will be elevated!

Takeaways:

1. Separation is a refining process.
2. Exposure may hurt, but the Lord exposes us to ourselves out of love. He will show us our foundation to build us back up.
3. When you go to the next level, some may think you've changed, and the reality is that you have. God has stripped you of your old ways and replaced it with something new. Don't forget where you came from, but don't dwell on it, either.

UNIT 4

Inadequacy

Unit 4

Inadequacy

You have made it to another unit. You should be so proud of yourself! While I know there are other things you could be occupying your time with, you are choosing to understand yourself more and grow in the word of God. That, my friend, is a form of discipline that you have mastered. In this unit, we are going to focus on things that make us feel inadequate. By the end of this lesson, you will know how to overcome when you feel like the odds are stacked against you. Before we begin, I want you to think about what the word *inadequate* means to you. Without looking up the definition, write what you think the word means.

Inadequate:

_____

_____

Now, I'm going to ask you a personal question, and I want you to be completely transparent. What makes you feel inadequate? When you have an answer, please write it below.

_____

_____

_____

I struggled with feeling inadequate for years. Through comparing myself to others, I was blocking my view to see the abilities God has given me. One time I was talking to an educator, and her comment took me by surprise. They were frustrated with the way their students were performing academically and stated, "I wouldn't be surprised if half of my class scored a 13 on their ACT." My heart sank in my chest. When I first took the ACT, I scored a 13, and the second time, I scored a 14. The words this specific educator mumbled hurt me to the core, because I remember how I felt when my scores came in. When my brother and I transferred to a new school district, we really saw how many academic gaps we had. For me, personally, I was two and a half grade levels behind my peers in the tenth grade when it came to math.

The thing that frustrated me the most was being surrounded by kids who had been given tools and resources since kindergarten. They didn't have to worry about the same problems I did. As I progressed through school, I noticed that I began to take on a "woe is me" mentality. I wanted people to feel sorry for me. I wanted a handout because I felt I had been cheated out of my education. I wanted to feel smart and look smart. I just wanted to blend in. I viewed my situation as a pair of glasses. If I were blindfolded and had to reach into a toolbox to grab one thing that could help me repair eyeglasses, what would I choose? Better yet, what if my choice of tools to fix my glasses were between tape, nails, and glue? I realized that it's not about the tools I was given or lack thereof, it's about how I make the best of crummy situations.

I was angry because I felt inadequate academically, but the ball was still in my court. What was I doing to make the best of my situation? Below, I want you to write about a time when you felt inadequate. How did you make the best of the situation?

_____

_____

_____

_____

_____

_____

_____

_____

_____

_____

_____

My sister in Christ, trust me when I tell you that God is getting ready to show you how qualified you are. Because you are His daughter, you'll always be qualified. We are going to read a familiar story in the Bible about a man named Moses. We share so many similarities with him, but I want you to focus on the confidence he builds within himself when he has a clear understanding of what God has called him to do. Please read Exodus 2:5–10.

When Moses reached his destination, they discovered he was what ethnicity (v. 6)?

❑ Egyptian
❑ Hebrew

A pharaoh is a ruler in Egypt. Based on verse 10, Moses became whose son?

❑   The queen's
❑   Pharaoh's daughter

If you selected that Moses was a Hebrew and he was adopted by Pharaoh's daughter, you are absolutely correct! Moses was born a Hebrew, or Israelite, which makes that his ethnicity; however, since he was raised by Egyptians, he took on their cultural traditions. Can you imagine the confusion this might have caused Moses once he found out who he really was? How do you think Moses felt once he knew his identity and saw his people being treated poorly?

_____
_____
_____
_____
_____

One thing we tend to do when we are faced with adversity is run. What happened in Exodus 2:11–15 that caused Moses to run away?

_____
_____
_____
_____
_____

Moses had many strikes against him, in his eyes. He was born into an ethnicity that was enslaved, yet he was raised by those who enslaved his people. When he saw the wrongdoings that were taking place, he was overcome by frustration and killed an Egyptian worker. Just when he thought no one noticed, people made it clear to him that they saw what had happened.

One thing I love about being a teacher is seeing the growth of students. At times it may be hard to see the end game, but the little steps in between are crucial. Sometimes you encounter students who qualify for special services because of a disability, and you are able to see their progress throughout the year. If I had a choice, I would want Moses to be in my classroom, because he has hidden gems inside. While some say disability, I say don't diss their ability. When God called Moses to lead the Israelites to freedom, he questioned his own abilities and worried about what others would think. One thing I want you to know, sister, is that when God calls you, He sees something great in you, and provision will be granted each step of the way. Moses was terrified to carry out the mission God had called him to. Using the CSB, please fill in the blanks to the scripture below:

Exodus 4:10: But Moses replied to the Lord, "Please, Lord, I have _____ been _____ either in the past or recently or since you have been speaking to your servant—because my _____ and my _____ are _____."

Wow! Can you believe it? In the educational world, Moses would possibly have qualified for speech services. I would love to see how much growth he would make with his speech and confidence if he were my student. Is there something in your life that is causing you to feel insecure about yourself? If so, I want you to make a list of what those things are.

My Insecurity	Reasons Why

Before the end of this session, we will address each of our insecurities and come up with a game plan on how to put them behind us so we can walk forward.

When I enrolled in my classes for college, I remember feeling like I wasn't going to make it. While the rest of my peers were entering college as sophomores, I was entering as a freshman and taking remedial classes. To this very day, on my college transcript, you'll find the courses Intermediate Algebra and Improvement in Reading Skills. I started to question whether I was smart enough to make it through school and oftentimes found myself asking the Lord, "Who am I?" I felt as if my presence on a college campus wouldn't even leave a mark.

Sister, I know sometimes we may feel like we are so small in this large world, but you are able to leave a mark on every place you step foot in. When you're marked by God, you leave an everlasting imprint on people's hearts. It doesn't matter how big or small the deed is. It matters whether you've impacted a person's life in a positive way. Below, you'll find a few challenges that I want you to complete. Some of the challenges may require you to go outside of your comfort zone, and that is perfectly fine. Before you select a challenge, I want you to pray to the Lord and ask Him how He wants you to impact someone's life this week. If God leads you to a new challenge that is not listed, embrace it and go for it! Once you know what challenges you want to do, record the challenge you've selected, what day you completed the challenge, how it made you feel, and how the other person reacts on the chart provided.

Here are the challenges:

1. Write an encouraging note to someone.
2. Ask three people how their days are going.
3. Say "Good morning" to someone you've never spoken to.
4. Give a positive affirmation to someone you've never spoken to.
5. Ask someone if you can assist them in any way.

Challenge	Day/Date	Personal Feelings	Recipient's Reaction

My friend, I want you to be at ease with the thought of facing challenges and stepping out of your comfort zone. When we simply ask God, "Who am I?" He quickly reveals Himself first and says, "I am." This strategy that God uses allows us to fix our eyes back on the Creator of all things instead of focusing on our shortcomings. I want you to pay attention to how precise the Lord is when Moses gets wrapped up in his circumstances. Please read Exodus 3:11–14.

Since our generation is hugely into technology, I want you to put yourself in Moses's shoes with the verses you just read. Think about what might be going through your mind and how you may be feeling. I want you to pretend that you and God are having an intense text message conversation about fulfilling what He has called you to do. How are you going to respond? Fill in your conversation in the text bubbles below.

Despite how we may feel sometimes, God will always let us know that He has our best interests at heart. Although I felt as if I lacked tools academically, God built my confidence and allowed me to walk out on top. I no longer looked at my circumstances as disadvantages; I looked at them as opportunities to let God's light shine. Yes, I was insecure about my intelligence, and yes, I was enrolled in remedial courses, but, all glory to God, I graduated cum laude from college in 2017. My sister, let the insecurities be a motivation to keep pushing, even when things don't make sense. Do not give up, because I Am sent you, and I Am loves you!

As promised, we are going to revisit the insecurities that you wrote earlier. Your homework assignment for the end of this unit is to find one scripture that counteracts each of your insecurities. For example, if my insecurity is not being qualified for a task, a scripture to counteract that thought is Romans 5:1, which tells me I'm justified by faith and have the peace of God through my Lord, Jesus Christ. That's something powerful to scream about! You are more than qualified, sister.

As you reflect on life, I want you to remember a few things:

1. When you feel inadequate, God will always show you who He is.
2. When the odds are stacked against you, know that God is always for you.
3. Because you are marked by God, you have influence in the world.
4. I Am sent you, and, I Am loves you.

Be blessed, and I will see you for our next unit.

UNIT 5

I'm Salty

Unit 5

I'm Salty

I remember the first time my daddy began to teach me how to drive. I would sit on his lap and turn the wheel of the riding lawn mower, embracing the smell of fresh-cut grass. I never quite got hold of the gas pedal until I was allowed behind the wheel of a real vehicle. Specifically, there was a time when my daddy took my brother and me driving around the block. My brother did such a great job using his turn signals and stopping at the appropriate time; on the other hand, I did awful! At ten years old, I got behind the wheel of a 2000 Dodge Durango. My seatbelt was on, the mirrors were adjusted, and I floored the gas pedal! I'm pretty sure my daddy wanted to jump out of his skin during that moment. The story is funny to me now, and when I sit back and analyze what's in a car, it makes me think of women as a whole.

The most important parts of a car are the windshield and the rearview mirror. While they both have the function of helping you see, one is meant to be looked through consistently, while the other is to be looked at periodically. I want you to picture your life as a car. If you were driving down the highway and decided to constantly look in your rearview mirror instead of through your windshield, you would miss what's happening in front of you and the exit to your destination. Honey, you are in the driver's seat of this thing called life, and so many times, we keep looking back instead of looking forward. In this unit, we will take a long journey to understand.

1. what is behind us,
2. what is in front of us,
3. what causes us to hesitate or stumble, and
4. how to avoid getting "salty."

My sister, when we look back, it brings up old feelings and sometimes causes us to get salty. As we go through this section together, I want you to be transparent with the Lord about what's holding you back. Write a prayer to Him about what you are expecting Him to reveal to you in this unit.

_____

_____

_____

_____

_____

_____

This unit will be a fairly hefty one, so I want to thank you in advance for being so committed to the readings and activities. We will be doing more character analysis than in previous units. Please read Genesis 18:20–33.

There is so much rich dialogue going on between God and Abraham here; however, Abraham seems to be extremely worried about what God is planning on doing to a specific set of cities.

What are the names of the cities (v. 20)?

_____

_____

Why are the cities being looked at by God (v. 20)?

_____

_____

Who is asking God questions about sweeping away the righteous people in the cities (v. 23)?

_____

_____

In verse 25, Abraham asks God a very bold question. Fill in the blanks using the CSB interpretation: Verse 25: "You could _____ possibly do such a thing: to _____ the _____ with the _____, treating the righteous and the wicked _____. You could _____ possibly do that! Won't the _____ of the _____ _____ do what is _____?"

At this point in the story, I can picture God having a little chuckle at Abraham. Have you ever watched a child try to boss his or her parents around? I'm picturing this scene playing out a little something like that. Abraham is very confused right now at the fact that God wants to get rid of the cities Sodom and Gomorrah. Abraham has a strong feeling in his heart that there may be some righteous people in the town. Before we move on, let's talk about the word *righteous*. In the blank below and without using a dictionary, write what you think the word righteous means.

Definition of Righteous:

_____

_____

Using our knowledge of root words, we can see a word that stands out in the word *righteous*, and that word is *right*. According to Merriam Webster, to be right [2]means to be correct, good, or appropriate. The suffix *-eous* [3]means to resemble or look. Let's put it all together! The word *righteous* means to "look appropriate." When we talk about looking appropriate, I want you to think back on unit 2, when we learned about how we were created in the image of God, acquiring character traits like those of the Father, Son, and Holy Spirit. We also learned about the importance of holding ourselves in a manner that resembles God. This includes our actions and choices. To be righteous simply means to be in right standing with God.

Abraham pleaded with God to find righteous people in the cities of Sodom and Gomorrah. Each time he came back to the Lord, it seemed like the numbers kept dropping drastically. Please read verses 26–33 and complete the chart below.

```
50 people (total number God said)
- 5 people
  _____
          (How many people are left?)
- 5 people
  _____
          (How many people are left?)
- 10 people
  _____
          (How many people are left?)
- 10 people
  _____
          (How many people are left?)
- 10 people
  _____
          (How many people are remaining?)
```

---

2   Right. In *The Merriam-Webster.com Dictionary*. Retrieved January 24, 2020, from https://www.merriam-webster.com/dictionary/right

3   -eous. In *The Merriam-Webster.com Dictionary*. Retrieved January 24, 2020, from https://www.merriam-webster.com/dictionary/-eous

With a total of ten people remaining from Abraham's count, how many do you think were found righteous? Let's look at Genesis 19:10–15 and complete the information below.

Write the names of the individuals mentioned in verses 10–15.

_____

_____

Who did Lot speak to about leaving with him and his family (v. 14)?

_____

_____

Why didn't the individuals Lot spoke to leave with him (v. 14)?

_____

_____

How many people were able to leave the city before it was destroyed (v. 15)?

_____

_____

When Lot asked his sons-in-law to travel with him and his family, his sons-in-law thought it was a joke and missed out on their blessing. The story ends with a total of four people who get to leave the city before it is destroyed. That's six fewer people than Abraham expected. Lot, his wife, and his two daughters were venturing toward new beginnings, but they had to leave their old life behind. Girlfriend, sometimes God calls us to something different, and it's up to us whether we follow Him or not. There was a time in my life when I was completely miserable at a job. I felt like an outcast and found myself suffering from depression for about four months. As soon as I pulled into the parking lot, I would get anxiety, and my chest would tighten up to the point where it was hard for me to breathe. In short, I was super salty! I repeatedly asked the Lord to remove me from that work environment, but it didn't happen the way I wanted it to.

One thing I learned about the Lord during that period of my life is that He operates on His time, and His deliverance looks different depending on the situation. Typically, we think deliverance comes in the form of being completely removed from a situation. Little do we know, our God has no limits and exceeds the boundaries set by man; thus, deliverance can also be obtaining the stamina, perseverance, change of heart, and mindset to make it through a situation with peace. God can either deliver us *out* or He can deliver us *through*, but either way, it's still deliverance. In the work scenario, God delivered me through the situation first. He had to work on me and change my mindset. Once I mastered that piece, He delivered me out of the situation. I was able to leave with all my work intact and my name in good standing. I walked away with a changed heart.

In Lot's case, God delivered his family out of the situation. Take a look at Genesis 19:16–17 and complete the activity below.

What did Lot do?

- ❏ He ran
- ❏ He fell
- ❏ He hesitated
- ❏ He screamed

What command did one of the angels give to Lot's family?

- ❏ Gather as many people as possible
- ❏ Run, don't look back, don't stop on the plain
- ❏ Stop when you get to the plain
- ❏ Go back and get your sons-in-law

Lot did what a lot of us do in our lives when it's time for us to go to our next destination: he hesitated. The King James and New King James versions use the word "lingered." The words used to describe Lot's actions are an interesting reminder of my childhood. My mother would always say "lollygagging": "Y'all quit that lollygagging and get where you need to be!" I think Lot would most likely hear that from my mother if he were in my household. Sister, so many times we hesitate to leave the past in the past. When we get to that point, it's difficult to move forward. I want you to think of something in your personal life that you're hesitating with. Why do you think you're hesitating?

_____

_____

_____

I know that, for me, I would always hesitate when it was time for me to move on to something new. Whether that was a relationship, a friendship, or a job, I would find myself lollygagging because I wasn't quite sure what was on the other side. Sometimes it would cause me to look back and dwell on the same situation God was trying to deliver me from. We just read in Genesis 19:17 that the angels gave Lot and his family a command, stating, "Run for your lives! Don't look back and don't stop anywhere on the plain! Run to the mountains, or you will be swept away!" (CSB). In the specific region where Lot and his family lived, there were five main cities located on the plain. The cities included Sodom, Gomorrah, Admah, Zeboiim, and Bela (known as Zoar). When the angels gave Lot and his family instructions on where to run, it was because the remaining three cities were to also be destroyed along with Sodom and Gomorrah. For now, I want you to focus on the city of Bela (Zoar). Please read Genesis 19:18–25 and complete the activities below.

Who is Lot pleading with?

❑ God
❑ The angels
❑ His wife

What is Lot afraid of? Check all that apply.

❑ Running to the mountains
❑ Dying
❑ Being overtaken by the disaster

Fill in the blanks in the following verses using the CSB.

Verse 20: "Look, this town is _____ _____ for me to flee to. It is a small place. _____ let me run to it—it's _____ a small place, _____ it? —so that I can survive."

Verse 21: And he said to him, "All right, I'll _____ your _____ about this matter too and will _____ _____ the town you mentioned."

Verse 22: "Hurry up! Run to it, for I cannot do anything until you get there." Therefore the name of the city is _____.

Uh-oh! We ran into a problem. Lot wanted to stop in a city that was located on the plain. Bela, or what we know as Zoar, was one of the five cities that was supposed to be destroyed. Lot's words truly hit home for me when he tells the angels that the town is "close enough" for him to "flee." Lot was not fully ready to leave his old life behind. He wanted to be as close as possible to his past because it was something he was familiar with. Sister, when we can't let go of our past, it puts us in the way of fire. In a previous relationship, I still wanted to be close enough to the person to be friends but not in a serious relationship with that person after the breakup. I was torn between my old life and my new life. Girl, sometimes we just need to cut all ties and not end up in the city of Zoar. It's too close to our past, especially when we are trying to move forward. I want you to do some soul-searching. What is the city of Zoar in your life that is close to your past and keeping you from reaching the mountains?

_____

_____

_____

I'm praying that the Lord builds you up to be strong, run past your city of Zoar, and head straight to the mountains. For the last part of this unit, we are going to focus on how to avoid being "salty." Please read Genesis 19:26–29.

What did Lot's wife do?

❏ She ran back
❏ She looked back
❏ She walked back

What were the consequences of her actions?

❏ She got angry
❏ She turned bitter
❏ She turned into a pillar of salt

Sister, she was literally salty, pun intended. She was not ready to leave her past behind, either. When we are SALTY, we tend to struggle with the following points:

1) Sentimental value
2) Attachment
3) Leaving
4) (Keeping) Tabs
5) Years

When we become SALTY, we can't move because we're stuck in the past. Using the chart below, I want you to be honest with yourself. What is making you SALTY, and how can you move forward?

SALTY	In your life, what is making you SALTY?	How can you move forward in each category?
Sentimental Value		
Attachment		
Leaving		
(Keeping) Tabs		
Years		

Sister, whenever you feel yourself getting SALTY, I want you to think about what each letter means. Although Lot and his wife had a hard time letting go, it doesn't mean that you will. No more can we hold onto the city of Zoar and put ourselves in the way of fire. We are bigger and better than that! In Jesus' name, amen. Now that we've reached the end of our unit, I think it's time for a good joke. How do you become salty? I'm not sure; ask Lot's wife.

UNIT 6

Me. We. He.

Unit 6

Me. We. He.

She felt her phone vibrate in her back pocket, and to her surprise, it was a friend she hadn't heard from in a while. When she read the message, her stomach dropped, her heart raced, and her eyes filled with tears. "Hey, some girl is claiming to be pregnant by the person you've been seeing." She didn't have anything to say on the phone except, "OK." The tears in her eyes got heavier and heavier, but she refused to let one drop. When she got home, she wanted it all to end. With pills lined up and alcohol near, she reflected on the situation. Suddenly, there was such a warm embrace. It was a hug. A hug from the Lord that told her everything was going to be "OK."

The story above touches my heart. As I typed this story, I hesitated, because the young lady who got the text message was me. We have made it to our last session, and you are in for such a great treat! As the book comes to an end, I want to tell you how thankful I am for your diligence. I have truly enjoyed working with you, and my prayer is that you will take what you've learned about yourself and share it with others for the glory of the Lord. My friend, it's time to move from *me* to *we* to *He*.

When I got the text message from my friend, obviously there were a plethora of emotions that arose, but from that situation, God still got the glory. I had two choices. I could either dishonor the parties involved and make it about me, or I could have a simple conversation with the parties involved and see where it would take us. I chose option two, and I saw firsthand how the Spirit of the Lord worked. You'd be surprised how powerful a simple conversation can be. The young lady and I talked about future goals, different foods we like, and how life can sometimes stink! In my eyes, the parties got the attention they were looking for. They experienced Christ's love for them, and I couldn't be mad at all! We talked about how we are able to forgive and love, just like Him. For the first time in my life, I finally understood what Luke 9:23 meant when it says, "Then he said to them all, 'If anyone wants to follow after me, let him deny himself, take up his cross daily, and follow me.'" I was finally able to die to my flesh.

From that moment, I knew my life wasn't about me. It wasn't about other people. It was all about Jesus. While this unit may look different from the rest, we will take a close look at the life of a person who happens to be near and dear to me. He's my best friend, and His name is Jesus! In the twenty-sixth chapter of Matthew, Jesus is nearing His time of death and has an important decision to make. The thing I love so much about Jesus is His authenticity. He knows what it's like to face temptation, to lose a loved one, to get bullied, to have haters, and to be stressed. When God saw the need for the world to have a Savior, He knew His Son had to come in the form of a human so that He could relate to us on every aspect while still exhibiting self-control to resist sin.

Turn to Matthew 26 and read verses 39, 42, and 44. The three verses have the same thing in common. What is Jesus asking God?

_____

_____

_____

_____

_____

_____

The cup that Jesus is talking about is death. Jesus had feelings just like us, and He was terrified of what was to come. He's asking God if there is any way for Him to escape death. The beautiful thing is when He says, "Your will be done." My friend, when we think of Jesus, we should always be reminded of His selflessness. Sometimes, when our emotions are at stake, we tend to look out for ourselves, but Jesus decided to look out for us! The word *love* is ambiguous. Love is a choice, and love is also an action. Please read 1 Corinthians 13:4–5. Have fun completing the word search based on the scripture, which speaks on what love is.

Word Bank	
Not rude	No record
Not boastful	Not self-seeking
Not irritable	Kind
Jesus	No envy
Not arrogant	Patient

N	O	T	S	E	L	F	S	E	E	K	I	N	G
N	E	T	S	N	O	N	T	R	B	O	S	N	A
N	R	E	E	U	J	E	S	U	S	B	S	O	R
E	E	O	E	D	R	O	C	E	R	O	N	E	V
T	B	L	S	N	O	E	N	V	Y	E	T	U	S
E	L	B	A	T	I	R	R	I	T	O	N	R	N
A	T	N	E	I	T	A	P	T	E	C	I	K	E
V	E	L	R	E	I	E	O	E	E	A	R	I	R
T	G	O	G	N	E	E	D	U	R	T	O	N	N
U	G	D	K	I	N	D	N	I	L	E	T	U	N
B	G	D	N	O	T	A	R	R	O	G	A	N	T
R	L	U	F	T	S	A	O	B	T	O	N	B	R
N	T	A	R	T	O	U	R	O	T	F	O	O	T
R	G	O	E	Y	S	I	R	O	T	B	N	N	E

Jesus's character traits are a perfect example of what love is. Jesus was never arrogant, boastful, or self-seeking, but he was always so patient, kind, and forgiving. In today's society, we live in a "What's in it for me?" type of world. My sisters, I want all of you to know that that mindset is dangerous. When we become so consumed with ourselves, we miss the opportunity to pour into others, which takes the glory away from the Lord. There's a five-letter word that explains what self-seeking truly is, and that is *pride*.

In order to move further in our ministry, we have to be able to see where pride lies in our hearts.

Sometimes it's evident, and sometimes it's hiding and we haven't noticed it yet. Jesus's ministry was never solely about Him; it was about dying for humanity so we could have hope in a new covenant that is to come with the Father. Jesus could have easily focused on himself in the garden of Gethsemane, but instead He aligned Himself with the will of the Father. In Jesus's response in obedience, you and I were saved. Our time here on earth should be a replica of the example Jesus set. The ministry is not about us; it's about impacting people for the glory of the Lord.

Thinking back on a time when I was in the classroom, one of my students hurt someone's feelings with the words he said. When I asked the student why he said those hurtful words, his response was, "I wasn't thinking about how he would feel. I was just mad." That comment alone shows the significance of why I teach pronouns in my classroom. Pronouns are used to take the place of a noun. For example, if I'm using a sentence that states, "Sarah likes to go shopping," a pronoun I could use in place of *Sarah* is *she*. This would then change the sentence to say, "She likes to go shopping." If Sarah were speaking, the pronoun that would be used is *I*, which changes the sentence to state, "I like to go shopping." In this next activity, we will use pronouns to identify Jesus's selflessness. Please read the scriptures below and circle each pronoun you see.

Matthew 26:39 (CSB): Going a little farther, he fell facedown and prayed, "My Father, if it is possible, let this cup pass from me. Yet not as I will, but as you will."

Matthew 26:42 (CSB): Again, a second time, he went away and prayed, "My Father, if this cannot pass unless I drink it, your will be done."

Jesus shifted from a *me* mindset to a *He* mindset, which included a *we* mindset. My friend, get ready—we're getting ready to do the same thing. I know many of us have heard the saying, "Pride comes before the fall," but did you know that that's actually scripture? Proverbs 16:18 states, "Pride comes before destruction, and an arrogant spirit before a fall" (CSB). The whole idea of disobedience and sin is not about the earthly categories we seem to put them in, but it's about self-gratification. Pride only focuses on the pronouns *I*, *me*, and *my*. Here's a quick heart check. PRIDE is present when we focus only on our

1. Position,
2. Relevance,
3. Idealism (Perfection),
4. Dignity, and
5. Ego.

You may be wondering how you can move past pride, and the answer is through humility. When we humble ourselves, God is able to work on the pride in our hearts. Remember, He trades us beauty for our ashes. We can overcome by being honest with the Lord and asking Him to open our eyes to see the bigger picture. Jesus was a very meek and submissive man. While our society has put a negative connotation on those words, I'm here to reassure you that *meek* simply means "patient," and *submissive* simply means "in agreement." These character traits didn't make Jesus weak; they made Him strong. He mastered what true love is through an agreement with His Father. I want you to write some scriptures about pride in your own words. Summarize each scripture below and think about how it connects to you.

Proverbs 11:2

_____
_____
_____
_____

Philippians 2:3

_____
_____
_____
_____

James 4:6

_____
_____
_____
_____

James 4:10

_____
_____
_____
_____

1 Peter 5:5

_____
_____
_____
_____

There's something about being humble that just moves the Lord's heart!

The same strength that Jesus has from the Spirit lives in us. When we shift from taking the focus off ourselves to focusing on lost souls in the world, the Lord can then work through us. Our job is to plant seeds in people's hearts by sharing the gospel. We are fishers of men who are called to let our lights shine! In Genesis 3:14–15, God made His master plan present for generations to come. What does the Lord say?

Genesis 3:15 (CSB): I will put _____ between you and the woman, and between your offspring and her offspring. _____ will strike your _____ and you will strike his _____.

These verses were a foreshadowing for who was to come—Jesus. Although we noted His emotions in the Garden of Gethsemane, He accomplished what God said in Genesis 3, "He will strike your head." The place where Jesus was crucified is called Golgotha (which means "place of the skull") (Matthew 27:33). By Jesus being obedient and dying on the cross, He struck the enemy's head. It's not a coincidence that Golgotha means "the skull."

While you still have time and breath in your body, I challenge you to take up your cross and die daily to pride. By Jesus setting the example for us, we were saved. Imagine how impactful we can be if we surrender our lives to Him. He came, He conquered, and He's coming back. Together, let's move from *me* to *we* to *He*. In Matthew 22, Christ issues a reminder to always love the Lord your God with all your heart, with all your soul, and with all your mind and to love others as we love ourselves. Sister, we still have time to pour into others just like Christ poured into us. Let's use this opportunity to let His light shine.

Revelation 22:20–21 (CSB): He who testifies about these things says, "Yes, I am coming soon." Amen! Come, Lord Jesus! The grace of the Lord Jesus be with everyone. Amen.